HIPSTER COOK BOOK

SPIFFING RECIPES

BY
TRACY CHOCOLATE

Red Cherry Books

Hipster Cook Book

Spiffing Recipes

By Tracy Chocolate

Published by Red Cherry Books
December 2017
WWW.REDCHERRYBOOKS.COM

Cover Design & Photography by Red Cherry Books
ISBN 978-1-911199-16-8
Copyright © Red Cherry Books

RED CHERRY BOOKS
81 Fernwalk, Ballincollig,
Cork, Ireland

CONTENTS

EASY STARTERS

Hipster omelettes——————3
Plucky dips——————5
Wild Gaucomole & Egg on toast——————5
Spiffing Smoothies——————7
Pickled Onions——————9
Totally Tomato Soup——————10
Savage Salads——————11
Reckless tomatoes, Salad People——12

FRESH MAINS

Bold Thai Stir Fry——————15
Skirt Beef & lime Tacos——————17
Old English Pork Sausages——————19
Chicken Curry——————20
Audacious Spaghetti Bolognese——21
Perfect Pizzas——————22
Fabulous Fajitas——————24
Quick Veggie Nachos——————25

COOL DESSERTS

Yummy Sour Cream Chocolate Cake—27
Rockin Raspberry Cream Cake——————29
Gingerbread Pack-Man——————30
Cheeky Chocolate Brownies——————31
Awesome Apple Cake——————32
Jumping Jelly Cheesecake——————33

I HOPE THAT YOU
ENJOY MAKING THE
RECIPES FROM
THIS BOOK. THE
MEALS ARE
SIMPLE, HEALTHY
AND FUN.

FOR OISIN AND MILO

CHARLIE, BETHANY, JUDE

PATRICK, ANASTASIA

JESSIE, RACHEL AND CIARA.

THE RECIPES HAVE
QUANTITIES WHICH
SHOULD FEED FOUR
PEOPLE. THE CAKES
WILL SERVE MORE THAN
FOUR PEOPLE. IF YOU
ARE VEGETARIAN OR HAVE
ALLERGIES, PLEASE
SUBSTITUTE ACCORDINGLY

EASY STARTERS

HIPSTER OMELETTES

Ingredients

1 tbsp (tablespoons) Extra Virgin Olive Oil

8 eggs

3 spring onions

200 g new potatoes

½ tsp of sage

4 rashers unsmoked bacon

100 g cheddar cheese

How to make

- Peel and thickly slice the potatoes, boil ing water for 10 minutes, then drain.

- Finely chop the spring onions. Slice the tomatoes.

- Grate the cheese.

- Snip the bacon into pieces with scissors, wash your hands.

- Break the eggs into a bowl, and whisk them up with a whisk or a fork. If you like you can add a little salt and pepper.

- Add half the cheese, the bacon, tomatoes, sage and spring onions to the mix and stir.

- Heat a frying with 1tbsp of olive oil, and when it is hot pour in the mixture.

- Gently stir a few times, scatter some more cheese on the top and then leave for 5 minutes when the base starts to cook. A good frying pan with a heavy base helps the omelette to cook slowly.

- It is cooked when the egg has set all the way through.

- Turn out of the pan, cut into slices and enjoy with some salad, or as breakfast.

Yolo Yoghurt Dips

Simple, healthy and easy dips and a change from mayonnaise. Just start with yoghurt and add your ingredients.
250 ml Greek or plain yoghurt

Carrot & Sweetcorn
Add 100 g grated carrot and 100 g sweetcorn (fresh is best, but tinned is ok)

Cheesy Dip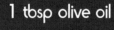
200 ml grated cheddar cheese

Raita Dip
Half a cucumber, finely chopped.
This is a good accompaniment to curry.

Pesto & Yoghurt Dip
2 tbsp green pesto
1 lemon (halved and squeezed for the juice)
1 tbsp olive oil

Wild Gaucamole

2 avocados
1 lemon
1 tbsp extra virgin olive oil
back pepper
Optional: 1 tomato, 1/8 of a red chilli pepper, 3 spring onions. All finely chopped.
•Half the avocadoes, take out the stone and then score the flesh. Squeeze out the chunks of flesh into a bowl.
•Put in a blender with the olive oil and pinch of pepper. Squeeze in the juice of lemon.
•If you haven't got a blender, make a delicious chunky gaucomole by mashing with a fork.
•Serve with tortilla chips, slices of toast, or carrot sticks. I love gaucomole on toast with an egg!
•Variations: add finely chopped tomato, a very small piece of finely chopped chilli (an 1/8 of a chilli pepper) and chopped spring onions.

DIPPING STICKS

2 carrots, peeled and cut into 'batons', long strips

Half a cucumber cut into strips

1 stick of celery, washed and cut into chunks

Breadsticks

Dry toast cut into strips

Tortilla chips

Ingredients - Mango Milk

2 mangoes
250 ml / 9 fl oz cold milk
2 tbsp caster sugar

ice cubes, or ice cream

Ingredients - Green Special

2 limes
Handful of fresh young spinach leaves
Two bananas, peeled and sliced.
Two kiwis, peeled and sliced.
Oat flakes, seeds, nuts

- Peel the mangos (or other fruit) and cut off as much flesh as you can around the stone. A lot of juice will run off so be sure to catch these in a bowl.

- Mash up the fruit pieces or put into a blender until smooth.

- If you want to make it more of a milkshake, add milk sugar either in the blender or in a jug and mix until thick and smooth.

- Add ice cubes to serve for a refreshing chilled drink, or as a decadent treat, add a scoop of ice cream and blend. Sprinkle with grated nuts, oat flakes or seeds.

Variations:

Swap the mangos for bananas, pineapples, kiwis or strawberries. Have fun experimenting!

PICKLED ONIONS

Ingredients

500g shallot onions

40g of salt

500ml malt vinegar

200g clear honey

1. Use any onion you like. Smaller shallots can be nice.
2. Wear goggles! It sounds silly, however it can really help to protect your eyes from streaming.
3. Place the onions in a saucepan, cover with boiling water and leave to cool.
4. Peel the onions. Clean them under water and cover with the salt.
5. Put them back in the saucepan with water and leave overnight.
6. The next day, take the onions out and rinse off the salt. Dry with a clean tea towel.
7. Cover them with honey by dipping them. Then put them back into a saucepan with the vinegar and the rest of the honey. Heat slowly until the honey is dissolved and switch off. Do not let it boil.
8. Pour out the onions and vinegar into airtight jars, leave open until they cool, then seal. Leave for one month or two to soften and pickle.

TOTALLY TOMATO SOUP

I MADE TOMATO SOUP WITH TINNED TOMATOES FOR AGES, AND IT WAS FINE. BUT ONE DAY I USED FRESH TOMATOES WITH VEGETABLES AND ROASTED THEM AND THE FLAVOUR WAS AMAZING. SO I'D RECOMMEND GIVING THIS A TRY. TO KEEP THE FAT LOW WHILST ROASTING YOU CAN ADD ONLY A SMALL AMOUNT OF EXTRA VIRGIN OLIVE OIL.

Ingredients

2 carrots

2 sticks celery

2 medium onions

4 cloves garlic

Extra virgin olive oil

1 vegetable stock cube

200 g tomato passata.

12 large ripe tomatoes

400 ml of water

salt

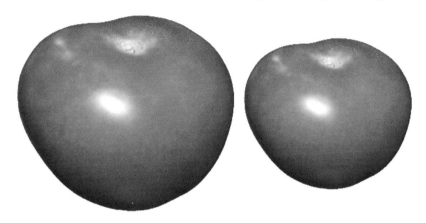

1. Put on the oven to Gas Mark 6/200c

2. Peel the carrots and onions, and roughly chop up. Slice the celery.

3. Take a large baking tray and add a couple of tablespoons of extra virgin olive oil, a pinch of salt and black pepper.

4. Add the tomatoes, carrots and onions to the tray and mix well with your fingers to make sure that all are covered in oil. Add the gloves of garlic with their skin on, no need to take these out.

5. Roast for 30 minutes, or until the tomatoes start to caramalise and the carrots and onions look soft and sweet.

6. Take these out of the oven. The tomatoes should have split, to being careful not to burn your fingers, carefully take off the skin. I put in a pan and bash these with a masher or spoon and that way the skin usually separates and I can scoop it out.

7. Bash the garlic cloves to release the roasted mushy garlic inside, and discard their skins.

8. Add the de-skinned tomatoes and garlic to a large pan. Add the roasted carrots, onions and sliced fresh celery.

9. Pour in 400 ml of boiling water, the stock cube and tomato passata.

10. Stir for a few minutes and bring to the boil.

11. Reduce the heat, cover with a lid and simmer for 20 minutes, or until the desired thickness.

12. You can mash for a lumpy texture, or put in a blender for a smooth taste.

13. Season to taste. Serve with crusty bread.

SAVAGE SALADS

Does salad feel dull to you? Do you have kids who won't touch it? Don't be put off trying if you think it is boring. There are some ways to try and make a salad more appealing. Try getting some of you, your friends or families favourite ingredients and be creative with how you put them together. Like tortilla chips? Olives? Cheese? Then crumbel up the tortillas, grate the cheese, slice the olives and mix up with lemon juice.

- Chop the salad really small. For example, tomatoes and cucumber, but in very small pieces. Make ribbons out of red cabbage, cucumber, carrots. Japanese style salads can be beautiful, spend a bit of time preparing.
- Include your child in what kind of salad you make. Get them to choose one thing that they do like, such as tomatoes. This can be mixed with cheese, another salad vegetable, as long as your child enjoys it.

- Salad can be anything, it doesn't have to be just leaves and a tomato. It could be mixed with potatoes, fruit, pasta, couscous or rice.

- Take your kids out shopping and get them to help you choose fruit and vegetables. Sometimes you may be too busy. But occasionally, take a bit longer to show your kids what is ripe. If they love pineapple, show them what a ripe fresh pineapple smells, looks and feels like. Include them in some of the preparation if they are old enough, and watch their enthusiasm grow.

Tuna, Egg & Spinach Salad

1 bag of fresh spinach
1 tin of tuna steak
4 eggs
Serve with:
Crusty rolls or pasta penne
Dressing:
75 ml extra virgin olive oil
50 ml white wine vinegar
1 tbsp grainy mustard

1. Poach the eggs either in an egg poacher (boil water, reduce slightly, then crack open the eggs in the water for 3-4 minutes) or in a saucepan.

2. Open the tuna, drain out the juice and flake.

3. Mix with the fresh spinach leaves and the dressing.

4. Serve on top of warm crusty bread or pasta (heated or cool). Break open the poached eggs so they are a well done, sticky but not hard consistency. Put one egg for each serving and eat straight away.

Salad people

Make salad faces or people. Leaves make good hair. Tomatoes or olives for eyes. Cucumber for noses and red pepper for the mouth.

The tomato is a fruit and contains carotene lycopene, one of the most powerful natural antioxidants.

Reckless tomato salad

4 ripe tomatoes at room temperature
A little salt
Extra virgin olive oil

Slice or chop the tomatoes depending on your preference. Drizzle with olive oil and a little salt. Simple but tasty.

STRAWBERRY, KIWI & GRAPE SALAD

Who doesn't like strawberries and grapes? They are naturally sweet but full of goodness too. Especially when the strawberries are in season. Let the strawberries come to room temperature by taking them out of the fridge one hour before. They really do taste better that way.

2 punnets of strawberries
1 large bunch of grapes
2 kiwi fruits
Fresh mint leaves (optional)
50 ml orange juice
1 tbsp sugar

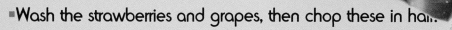

- Wash the strawberries and grapes, then chop these in half.

- Take off the skin of the kiwis, then slice.

- Mix all of this in a bowl in the orange juice and sugar

- Serve with fresh mint leaves (optional).

CARROT STRIPS, CHEESE AND GRAPE SALAD

1 carrot	**Dressing:**
1 bunch of grapes	2 tbsp mayonnaise
100 g Cheddar cheese	2 tbsp yogurt
	2 tbsp lemon juice

- Peel the carrots until the skin is off, and chop the bottom off. Carry on peeling into thin wide strips.

- Half the grapes. Cut the cheese into small cubes

- Make the dressing by combining the yogurt, mayonnaise and lemon juice and then mix up with the grapes, cheese and carrot strips.

- Ready to serve.

FRESH MAIN MEALS

BOLD THAI STIR FRY

Ingredients

2 tbsp Extra Virgin Olive Oil
250 g beef strips or steak cut into thin strips
2 tbsp oyster sauce or thai sauce
Half a red chilli, deseeded and finally chopped
2 peppers, (red and green) thinly sliced.

2 cups basmati rice

1. Put on the rice. Measure double the amount of water as rice in a pan, then bring to the boil with the lid on and simmer on a low heat. Total time to cook should be 15 minutes. Leave the lid off after it has cooked for the rice to dry and get fluffy.

2. While the rice is cooking, heat a large frying pan or wok with oil.

3. Add the beef and chilli. Keep on a medium sizzling heat, stirring all the time. Cook for about 10 minutes.

4. When the meat is browned, add the peppers for 1 minute.

5. Add the oyster sauce and cook for a further 2 minutes or until the beef is cooked through.

6. Scoop the rice into a small bowl, put a plate over the top and then tip over to get a nice 'round' rice shape. Scoop on the beef stir fry and serve straight away.

Skirt Beef & Lime Tacos

Ingredients

1 lb Skirt Steak, cut into 5 inch strips

Marinade:

2 garlic cloves, chopped.

4 tbps extra virgin olive oil

1 medium jalapeno, thinly sliced

2 limes, zest and juice

Tacos:

1 Little Gem Lettuce

2 avocados, sliced.

5 tomatoes on the vine, chopped.

3 Spring onions, thinly sliced.

8 taco shells or corn tortillas

1 small tub of sour cream

1. Mix the jalapeno, olive oil, garlic, limes and salt / pepper to taste to make a marinade. Slice the skirt steak into strips and mix together in a bowl and cover with cling film. Keep in the fridge overnight.

1. Put some extra virgin olive oil in a large frying pan. Over a high heat, brown the steaks on both sides for one minute. Then cook according to their weight and how rare you like them. Approximately 3 minutes (rare) to 6 minutes (well done) each side. TIP - for juicy steaks, leave out at room temprature for 30 minutes before cooking.

2. Rip up handfuls of lettuce, chop the tomatoes and spring onions.

3. If you like, add sour cream, gaucomole and tomato salsa.

Home Made Old English Pork Sausages

Ingredients

6 ounces organic lean pork, minced

2 ounces pork belly, minced

2 ounces fresh white breadcrumbs

1 onion, peeled & chopped finely or grated.

Small lemon rind (unwaxed) finely grated.

Fresh or dried sage, small handful

Fresh ground black pepper

Pinch of salt

2 eggs, beaten

1 ounce butter

1 tablespoon oil

2 tablespoons of flour

1 Egg white

- Mix the minced pork and pork belly in a large bowl with a wooden spoon.

- Add the seasoning, the pepper, salt, sage, lemon, onions and breadcrumbs.

- Add the two eggs and mix well. Really stir it!

- Chill the mixture in the fridge for an hour or two.

- On a large wooden board, scatter with flour. Put the egg white in a bowl.

- Take a small amount of sausage mix and roll into a ball, and a sausage.

- Dip it into the egg white and roll lightly in the flour. Put on a plate.

- Do the same with the rest of the mixture until you have made all the sausages.

- Now cook them in a large frying pan, or barbecue. Heat the butter and oil and cook until they are thoroughly done, there is no pink in the middle. It will vary depending on the size of sausage, but about 15 minutes. They will need turning to make sure they are brown evenly.

- Serve with kale and mashed potatoes, and thick onion gravy.

CHICKEN CURRY

WHO DOESN'T LOVE CHICKEN CURRY? THEY ARE VERY VERSATILE DISHES, AND YOU CAN ADD OR TAKE AWAY INGREDIENTS TO SUIT YOU. TRY A MORE TOMATO TASTE BY ADDING TINNED CHOPPED TOMATOES INSTEAD OF YOGURT.

Ingredients

1 large onion, finely chopped

2 garlic cloves, finely chopped

1 teaspoon fresh ginger, grated or finely chopped

1 tsp ground coriander

1 tsp garam masala

1 tsp ground cumin

3 to 4 chicken breasts

1. For the tastiest chicken curries, it's best to fry the seasoning and sauce and marinate for as long as possible. Preferably overnight. If that is not possible it will still taste good if you cook from fresh.

2. Day before. Heat the oil in a heavy based pan and fry the onions gently. They should 'sweat it out' slowly rather than burn. Add the garlic, ginger, coriander, garam masala and cumin and cook for a couple of minutes to allow the flavour to come out.

3. Mix the seasoning with half of the greek yogurt, cover the raw chicken to marinate and stick in the fridge overnight.

4. The next day, take the marinated chicken out. Take the heavy based pan again and heat a little oil, then add the chicken over the gentle heat. Stir the chicken to ensure it doesn't stick for about 10 minutes.

5. Pour in 200ml of boiling water and simmer for 30 to 40 minutes with the lid off, or until the water has 'reduced' (steamed away) and left a good thick sauce.

6. Cook the rice, put double the amount of water as rice in a pan, then bring to the boil with the lid on and simmer. Total time to cook should be 15 minutes. Leave the lid off after it has cooked for the rice to dry and get fluffy.

7. At the same time, boil or steam your accompanying vegetables, whichever ones your child will eat, and peas are often a good option and only take a few minutes from frozen.

8. Stir in the remaining yogurt, heat gently. Serve with basmati rice, and side vegetables.

AUDACIOUS SPAGHETTI BOLOGNESE

THE SECRET TO GOOD BOLOGNESE IS GOOD, LEAN FRESH MINCE. IT ALWAYS GOES DOWN A TREAT WITH KIDS.

Ingredients

1 tbsp olive oil

200 g lean or round steak mince

100 g button mushrooms, sliced

1 carrot, grated or finely chopped.

1 tin chopped tomatoes

Vegetable stock cube

2 tbsp tomato purée

Mixed herbs or fresh parsley to garnish

250 g spaghetti

BOLOGNESE SAUCE, ALSO KNOWN AS 'RAGU' IS A MEAT BASED SAUCE FROM BOLOGNA ITALY. HOWEVER IT IS NOT TRADITIONALLY SERVED WITH SPAGHETTI IN BOLOGNA OR ITALY!

1. Heat the olive oil in a large heavy based frying pan or saucepan. Add the mince and fry for 5 minutes until it is browned.

2. Add the carrots and mushrooms and cook for a further couple of minutes.

3. Add the tin of tomatoes and tomato puree.

4. Bring a pan with plenty of water to the boil.

5. Fill the empty tin of tomatoes half way with water, then add to the mince. Add the vegetable stock cube and mixed herbs if they are dried (wait until the meal is nearly cooked if they are fresh).

6. I half the spaghetti to make it easier to eat. Add these to the pan of water which should have a good 'rolling' boil. Reduce the heat and simmer for 15 minutes, or until the spaghetti,when it is snapped open has no 'dot' in the middle, and is cooked but not over cooked and losing its shape.

KIDS CAN ROLL OUT THE PIZZA BASE, AND HAVE FUN PUTTING ON THEIR OWN TOPPINGS. BELLISSIMO!

Ingredients

For the pizza dough
500 g of strong white bread flour
7 g sachet of yeast
2 tbsp of olive oil
300 ml warm water
Or feel free to use the ready made pizza mixes available in shops.

For the sauce
1 tbsp tomato puree
400 ml chunky passada
For the toppings
Ham, cut into small squares
Red/green peppers, cut into slices
Black or green olives, cut into slices
Mozzarella and cheddar cheese, grated
3 Tomatoes

1. Take a large mixing bowl, and put the yeast, olive oil, warm water and flour in and stir with a wooden spoon. It should make a sticky dough.

2. Take some flour and dust a large work surface. Take out the dough and stretch it out and then squash again into a round shape, 'work' the dough like this for about 10 minutes. Try to make the dough sooth and elastic. Then divide the dough up into two even sized balls, or four for smaller pizzas. Brush with a little olive oil and cover with cling film. Leave somewhere warm and wait until it has double in size, about 20 minutes.

3. Meanwhle, make the tomato sauce by mixing the puree with chunky passata. Heat the over to 200c/gas 7.

4. Cut up all the toppings into slices or squares, the ham, peppers, olives, tomatoes and grate the cheese.

5. Roll out the dough balls one by one with some flour. Line some baking trays with baking paper or brush with olive oil and pu the pizza bases onto them.

6. Spoon on the tomato sauce.

7. Now you can get creative! Put on the toppings that you like, spreading evenly. You can drizzle a little bit of olive oil over the top if you like, or scatter a little bit of fresh or dried herbs such as basil and oregano.

8. Cook in the oven for 12-15 minutes or until golden around the edges and the cheese is fully melted.

9.Serve with a green salad, garlic bread, coleslaw or on its own.

PIZZA
IS A LATIN AND
GREEK WORD MEAN-
ING TO PRESS AND
SOLID. THE LARGEST
PIZZA EVER CONTAINED
NEARLY 20,000 LBS OF
FLOUR AND WEIGHED
51, 257 LBS.

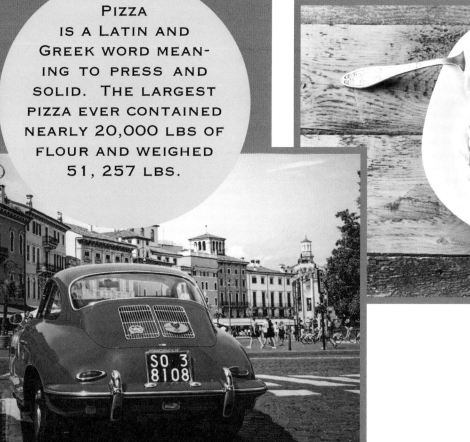

Fabulous Chicken Fajitas

Hola Amigos! This is a fun and tasty Mexican dish. Flour tortillas are used to wrap around spicy chicken and pep-

Ingredients

4 chicken breasts
Olive oil to fry
1 red pepper
1 yellow pepper
Tin of chopped tomatoes
Fajita seasoning
4 tomatoes
2 spring onions
2 ripe avocados
1 lemon
6-8 tortillas

1. Chop the peppers.

2. Cut the chicken breasts into even sized pieces.

3. Fry the chicken and peppers in a little olive oil, until the chicken has no pink and is well done, about 10 - 15 minutes.

4. Add the fajita seasoning, with the recommended water on the packet and half a tin of chopped tomatoes. Mix well.

5. If you like other toppings, add these now. Grate some cheese in a bowl.

6. Chop up 4 tomatoes, two spring onions and mix with the other half of the tin of tomatoes to make a simple salsa.

7. Slice open the avocadoes by cutting them in half, taking out the stone, then scoring along in a criss cross and squeezing the avocado out.
   Mix with a little lemon juice and mash for a chunky quacamole.

8. Warm up the tortillas either in the oven or microwave, according to the packet instructions.

9. Lay out the tortilla, choose your toppings, roll up and enjoy!

Fajitas are from Mexico. The word 'faja' is Spanish for a strip or belt, 'fajita' means little meat strips.

Ingredients

Nachos:

1 big bag of Corn Tortillas

4 garlic gloves, sliced thin, raw

2 Limes, zest and juice

8 tomatoes, chopped

1 medium jalapeno, sliced thinly

Toppings:

200g cheddar, grated

4 avocados, mushed with a fork

1 small tub of sour cream

1. Throw the corn tortilles into a big plate that can fit into the microwave. Stack them up with the mixed garlic, tomatoes, limes and jalapeno.

2. Sprinkle the top with grated cheddar cheese.

3. Heat for 1 minute in the microwave. Be careful with the cheese it might be very hot.

4. Serve with a small dish of sour cream and gaucomole.

COOL DESSERTS

YUMMY SOUR CREAM CHOCOLATE CAKE

Ingredients

For the cake

200 g plain flour

200 g caster sugar

50 ml water

1 tsp baking powder

40 g best-quality cocoa powder

175 g butter at room temperature

2 eggs

2 tsp vanilla extract

150 ml sour cream

For the icing

75 g butter at room temperature

75 g cocoa powder

300 g icing sugar

125 ml sour cream

1. Preheat the oven to Gas Mark 4/180°C.

2. Mix the butter, eggs, sugar, vanilla extract and sour cream together in a mixing bowl. Sieve the flour and cocoa powder into the bowl. Mix well with spoon or an electric whisk utnil the mixture is creamy. If it feels too dry and stiff, add up to 50ml of water.

3. Line two 20cm cake sandwich tins with baking paper. Place the mxture in both of the tins.

4. Bake for 35 minutes. Don't open the oven for at least 30 minutes otherwise the cake may collapse and not rise.

5. When the cake is ready (test with a knife to see if it comes out clean), take it out and leave to cool.

6. Make the icing in a large bowl. Put in all the ingredients and mix together well.

7. Spead some of the icing in the middle of the cakes, and place together. Spead the rest on the top.

8. You can deocrate with strawberries, or kiwis sliced. Either way it is delicious.

Rockin Raspberry Cream Cake

THE RASPBERRY IS FROM THE ROSE FAMILY. THERE ARE BLACK, BLUE, PURPLE AND YELLOW RASPBERRIES AS WELL AS THE MORE COMMON RED COLOUR. IT IS A GOOD SOURCE OF VITAMIN C.

Ingredients

For the cake

175 g self-raising flour
1 tsp baking powder
3 eggs
175 g caster sugar
175 g butter at room temperature
1 tsp vanilla extract

For the topping

100 g raspberries to decorate
3 tbps raspberry jam
150 g mascarpone cheese
100 g double cream
1 tbsp caster sugar

1. Pre heat the oven to Gas Mark 3/160c

2. Mix in the eggs and sugar into a mixing bowl. Sieve in the flour into the bowl. Add the baking powder, vanilla extract and softened butter.

3. Mix with a wooden spoon or electric whisk. The mixture should drop easily off a spoon. If it is too stiff, add 2 tbsp of water.

4. Line with baking paper two round cake tins, 20cm wide. Divide the mixture into the two.

5. Place in the oven for 35 minutes, don't open the door until this time.

6. You can tell if the cake is cooked by putting a knife, if it comes out clean it is cooked.

7. Turn out the cakes onto a cooling rack.

8. Whisk the mascarpone cheese, cream and sugar into a large bowl. This may take several minutes to get a good texture, or use an electric whisk.

9. When the cake is cool. Spread the raspberry jam in the middle and put the cakes together.

10. Spread the cream and cheese mixture on the top and decorate with raspberries.

Ingredients

350 g plain flour
1 tsp bicarbonate of soda
2 tsp ground or chopped ginger
125 g butter
175 g light soft brown sugar
1 free-range egg
4 tbsp golden syrup

To decorate

writing icing
Smarties

Pac-Man is an arcade game from 1980. Each 'ghost' has it's own personality, created to stop the game from being boring or impossible to play. The ghosts were called Blinky, Pinky, Inky and Clyde.

1. Sift together the flour, bicarbonate of soda, ginger and cinnamon and pour into the bowl of a food processor. Add the butter and blend until the mix looks like breadcrumbs. Stir in the sugar.

2. Lightly beat the egg and golden syrup together, add to the food processor and pulse until the mixture clumps together. Tip the dough out, knead briefly until smooth, wrap in cling film and leave to chill in the fridge for 15 minutes.

3. Preheat the oven to Gas Mark 4/180C. Line two baking trays with greaseproof paper.

4. Roll the dough out to a 0.5 cm thickness on a lightly floured surface. Use a round cutter for the pac-men, and cut out the mouth. The ghosts are harder, either use a 'tulip' cutter, or a round cutter and cut a wavy bottom. Place on the baking tray, leaving a big gap between them as they can spread.

5. Bake for 12-15 minutes, or until lightly golden-brown. Leave on the tray for 10 minutes and then move to a wire rack to finish cooling. When cooled put on icing sugar for the eyes. Ready to gobble up the smarties!

1. Cut up the butter into cubes. Break the dark chocolate into small pieces and put this and the butter into a heat proof bowl. Fill a saucepan, bigger than the bowl, with water (about quarter one third full).

2. Bring the ban to the boil slowly, stirring the butter and chocolate until they have melted.

3. Turn on the oven to Gas Mark 4 / 180C.

4. Take a shallow 20 cm baking tin and line with baking paper.

5. Sieve the plain flour and the cocoa powder into a mixing bowl.

6. Chop the milk chocolate into chunks on a board. This can be tricky as the chocolate can be hard. If you cut using the tip of the knife on the board, and then bringing the blade down.

7. Break 3 eggs into a mixing bowl, with the sugar. Mix with a whisk or electric mixer until it is thick and creamy.

8. Pour the cooled chocolate mixture over this mixture and fold together with a wooden spoon, or better still a rubber spatula.

9. Sieve the flour and cocoa powder onto the mixture. Fold in as before until the mixture is quite thick. Now mix in the milk chocolate chunks and marshmallows.

10. Pour the mixture into the tin. Bake in the oven for 25 minutes. Take out when the time is up and leave to cool. Then cut into squares to serve.

THE GREATEST NUMBER OF LAYERS IN A CAKE IS 230. IT WAS MADE IN AMERICA IN 2006.

Ingredients

200 g butter

150 g best dark chocolate

100 g plain flour

40 g cocoa powder

50 g small marshmallows

50 g milk chocolate

3 large eggs

250 g golden caster sugar

AWESOME APPLE CAKE

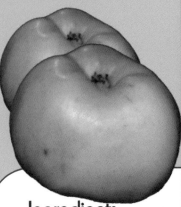

Ingredients

3 bramley apples
100 g butter at room temperature
175 g self raising flour
150 g caster sugar
1 tsp baking powder
1 tsp vanilla extract

1. Pre-heat the oven to Gas Mark 4 / 180c

2. Mix the sugar, eggs and butter in a large mixing bowl.

3. Sieve in the flour, baking powder and add the vanilla extra. Whisk or mix the ingredients until they are a goey consistency, quite thick.

4. Line a 20cm cake tin with baking paper.

5. Peel the apples and cut the flesh into small bite size chunks.

6. Mix them in with the mixture and pour into the cake tins.

7. Cook for 45 - 55 minutes or until nice and brown on the top. Don't check the cake for at least half an hour. Leave to cool oon a wire rack.

8. Tastes lovely still a bit warm, with custard or cream.

Ingredients

125 g ginger nut biscuits, bashed into crumbs
80 g butter at room temperature
1 lemon
200 g cream cheese
1 tin of evaporated milk
100 g caster sugar
2 packets of jelly, lemon and orange

1. Break up the lemon jelly and mix with 100 ml of boiling water in a jug. Even if it says more on the packet, just add this amount. Mix until the jelly dissolves. If it doesn't, put the jug in the microwave for 30 seconds and mix again. Leave to cool.

2. Break the ginger nut biscuits by hand, then place into a sandwich or clear plastic bag. Put on a chopping board, take out the rollinng and bash them with the long or side edge until they are fine bread crumbs.

3. Put the crumbed biscuits into a mixing bowl with the butter and give a good stir.

4. Line a 20cm cake tin with baking paper. If you have a tin with a removal bottom this will really help later on when you come to take the cheesecake out of the tin. If not, line the tin and up around the sides with baking paper so that you can light it out later.

5. Take the biscuit crumbs and press firmly into the bottom of the tin and put in the fridge.

6. Next take the cream cheese and evaporated milk. Put these into a mixing bowl. Add the sugar. Cut the lemon in half and squeeze in the juice. Mix by hand or electric whisk until light and fluffy.

7. Pour in the cooled jelly and mix with a spoon. Add this to the top of the cake tin and crumbed biscuit and put in the fridge for 3 hours.

8. After 2 hours, break open the second pack of jelly and again mix with100 ml of boiling water in a jug until it dissolves. Leave to cool for 1 hour.

9. Lightly touch the top of the cheesecake to see if it has set. Pour in a little of the second cooled jelly mix. If it breaks the surface then leave this a bit longer. If it stays on top, which it should, pour on top of the cheesecake.

10. Put back in the fridge and leave to set for 2 hours.

11. When the jelly has set, take out of the fridge and carefully release the tin or lift out the baking paper and cheesecake.

Photo Credits